Prehistoric Stru[ctures of] Central Am[erica:]
Who Erected Them?

Martin I. Townsend

Alpha Editions

This edition published in 2024

ISBN 9789361476198

Design and Setting By

Alpha Editions
www.alphaedis.com

Email - info@alphaedis.com

As per information held with us this book is in Public Domain.
This book is a reproduction of an important historical work.
Alpha Editions uses the best technology to reproduce historical work
in the same manner it was first published to preserve its original nature.
Any marks or number seen are left intentionally to preserve.

INTRODUCTION.

It was not a long period after 1492, when the great Italian navigator with his Spanish crew made their first discoveries upon the central portion of America, that the Europeans, who had followed the footsteps of Christopher Columbus, began to fall in with structures of great magnitude and architectural beauty scattered widely throughout Mexico, Guatemala and Yucatan, &c.; and when the conquest of Peru was achieved, artificial highways and water courses were found there, such as could have owed their existence to no people but one with advanced knowledge of science as well as of the arts of civilized life. No people existed then upon this continent capable of doing the work which so astonished the world.

Thinking men and dreaming men have, from the earliest of these discoveries, been busying themselves to find out when, and by what people, these early monuments to human efforts were constructed.

Norwegian discoverers and Welsh emigrants have been pressed into the service. Our own Donnelly has changed the place where God and history had located the origin of the human race in the valley of the Tigris and Euphrates, to a suppositious island in the Atlantic Ocean, and led out the nations of the earth from there to Asia, Africa and western Europe, until he had no further need of the island and then sunk it in "the bottom of the sea."

A whole people have been pressed into the service of explaining this mystery. The convenient "Lost ten tribes of the House of Israel" have been set to do this work, as their fathers were compelled to "make brick without straw" in the Land of Egypt, and then suffered to escape to some land where search for them would be in vain.

The following treatise is written for the purpose of showing—

FIRST.—That the lands where these structures exist were known to commercial people and to many of the scholars of the countries about the Mediterranean Sea for at least a thousand years before the Christian Era.

SECOND.—That these discoveries were made by the people of Phœnecia, originally located on the eastern border of the Mediterranean Sea, and by their colonies settled about Carthage in Africa, and throughout Spain and Portugal up to the Ebro; and who traversed every ocean almost as thoroughly as have their Anglo Saxon successors for the past four hundred years.

THIRD.—That the origin of the people who made these structures is shown, to absolute certainty, by the character of the architecture and by the character of the religious belief exhibited upon the temples which were erected to Baal, or Moloch, i. e. the Sun, who was their God, who was worshiped by the immolation of their infant children upon his altars.

This is proven as fully by the carvings and frescoes in Mexico and Guatemala, and by the stone circle of Sillustani, in the high country of Peru, and the figures inscribed upon the great entrance to the cemetery of Tiahuanuco in the same region, as if a thousand witnesses arose from the dead and testified before us.

PREHISTORIC CENTRAL AMERICA AND PERU.

THE ANCIENT GREEK AND ROMAN SCHOLARS KNEW OF THE EXISTENCE OF THE WESTERN CONTINENT.

In the earlier existence of the Greek and Roman peoples, knowledge was extremely limited. These peoples were without any mode of perpetuating or transmitting knowledge until the days, a little more than a thousand years before the Christian Era, when Cadmus brought from Phœnecia the letters which had been invented and adopted there for the representation and expression of articulate sounds; and by the combination of these letters to transmit and perpetuate human ideas. There is scarce a race of savages in our day where the mass of the body politic are as profoundly ignorant as were the great body of the Greek people a thousand years before Christ.

Even those men who made such acquisitions of knowledge as were possible in that day, could only learn from the lips of their imperfectly trained teacher, and by travel to those countries which the barbarous condition of the world allowed them to visit; and even after the learned men of the Greek Islands came to know the power of letters, how small must have been the amount of knowledge existing in the world, and how slow must have been its spread amongst the untaught commonalty of the then Greek world? In the day when the Phœnician ship Argo made a voyage to Colchis, at the east end of the Black Sea, it so fired the imagination of the Greek poets that they dreamed of the voyage and composed poems about it for centuries.

Indeed it was not until the Romans, just before the Christian Era, had subdued all the borders of the historic Mediterranean Sea, that free intercourse amongst the inhabitants prevailed. Up to that period every people, as a rule, carefully guarded all knowledge of their own wealth, and of their own acts and possessions from the rest of mankind, instead of making public expositions to attract the attention of the outside world to their useful achievements, and they sometimes passed laws for inflicting the severest punishments upon citizens who should reveal to the outside world the locations, nature, or extent, or value of their possessions.

Still, we glean from the ancient writers the following announcements.

1. That ancient book entitled "The Book of Wonders," ascribed to Aristotle, contains the following: "When the Carthagenians, who were

masters of the western ocean, observed that many traders and other men, attracted by the fertility of the soil and the pleasant climate, had fixed there their homes, they feared that the knowledge of this land should reach other nations, a great concourse to it of men from the various lands of the earth would follow, that the conditions of life, then so happy on that island, would not only be unfavorably affected, but the Carthagenian Empire itself suffer injury, and the dominion of the sea be wrested from their hands; and so they issued a decree that no one, under penalty of death, should thereafter sail thither." This passage is quoted, not merely with a claim that it refers to the Continent of America, but for the purpose of showing how carefully the Phœnician people, whether Asiatic, Carthagenian, or Spanish, guarded from the great world the foreign discoveries which they had made, and where their kindred were enjoying prosperity; and to enable us to see how little likely their discoveries would be to come to the knowledge of the great mass of mankind.

2. Let us look for a moment at some of the things which the ancient Greek and Latin authors have said indicating their knowledge of the existence of a western continent. Crates, a commentator on Homer, is quoted by authority of Strabo, a very learned author of the century before Christ, as saying that Homer means in his account of the western Ethiopians the inhabitants of the Atlantis or the Hesperides, as the unknown world of the west was then variously called.

3. Pliny also 6: 31-36, locates the western Ethiopians somewhere in the Atlantic. This shows that Crates and Pliny believed that the great poet Homer believed in the existence of a great continent on the western shore of the Atlantic ocean.

4. Plato says in his Timaeus, Chapter VI.: "The sea" (the Atlantic ocean), "was indeed navigable and had an island fronting the mouth which you in your tongue call the Pillars of Hercules, and this island is larger than Libya and Asia put together, and there is a passage hence for travelers of that day to the rest of the islands, as well as from those islands to the whole opposite continent that surrounds the real sea.

5. Humboldt quotes that Anaxagoras, who was born five hundred years B. C., and was a most eminent Greek philosopher, speaks of the grand division of the world beyond the ocean.

6. Aelian in his Variæ Historiæ, Book 3, Chapter 18, cites Theopompus, an eminent Greek historian, born about three hundred years B. C., as stating that the Meropians inhabit a large continent beyond the ocean, in comparison with which the known world was but an island.

7. Aristotle says in Chapters 84 and 85: "Beyond the Pillars of Hercules, they say that an inhabited island was discovered by the Carthagenians, which abounded in forests and navigable rivers and fruits of all kinds, distant from the continent many days' sail. And while the Carthagenians were engaged in making voyages to this land, and some had even settled there on account of the fertility of the soil, the Senate decreed that no one thereafter, under penalty of death, should voyage thither." Aristotle was born three hundred and eighty-four years before Christ.

8. Diodorus of Sicily, who lived in the century preceding the Christian Era, says in his Book 5,—19 and 20, that it was the "Phœnicians instead of the Carthagenians who were cast upon a most fertile island opposite Africa, where the climate was that of perpetual spring, and that the land was the proper habitation for gods rather than men."

He speaks of the continent, however, at length and with great detail, enumerating its fertile valleys and navigable rivers, its rich and abundant fruits and supply of game, its valuable forests and its genial climate.

9. Pliny quotes Statius Sebosus, in his volume 2, page 106, Bohn, as saying that *the two Hesperides are forty-two days' sail from the coast of Africa.*

THE PHŒNICIAN PEOPLE WERE EQUAL TO THE DISCOVERIES ON THE WESTERN CONTINENT, IF WE JUDGE THEM BY WHAT THEY ACTUALLY ACCOMPLISHED.

The prophet Isaiah, writing soon after seven hundred and fifty years before Christ, in the twenty-third chapter of his prophecy, gives us a pretty good idea of the unlimited commerce and the unlimited prosperity of the merchants of Tyre. Among other things he says the following, speaking of the City "*Whose antiquity is of ancient days.*" He calls the City "The Crowning City," "whose merchants are princes, whose traffickers are the honorable of the earth." The wealth and luxury of Tyre was eternally injurious to the Jewish people from the time of their return from Egypt to Canaan to the carrying away of Israel to Babylon in the later days. The Jewish husbandman, dazzled by the luxuries of Tyre and Sidon, was affected as those in more moderate circumstances are in later days, by the manners and customs of their rich neighbors, and were building groves in high places under which to worship, as did the priests of Baal in Palestine, and under the oaks in the northwest of Europe, where they acquired the name of Druids. They forsook the God of Abraham, Isaac and Jacob and worshipped Baal and Ashtaroth and Astarte, the Phœnician Venus.

They even sacrificed their children to Moloch, the relentless fire god, as Baal appeared in his sterner characteristics. But upon the loss of wealth which Phœnicia sustained in the wars with Nebuchadnezzar and subsequently with Alexander, the Phœnicians ceased to be conspicuously wealthy and luxurious, and Israel was left to worship that God who called their father Abraham from upper Chaldea, and who afterwards brought him out of the "House of Bondage" in Egypt after having been four hundred years enslaved there.

We have now glanced at the widespread influence of the Phœnician people over the borders of the Mediterranean sea and over the west and northwest of Europe.

Let it be remembered that what we have said upon this subject is founded upon authentic evidence from ancient history and modern fact.

Let us look for a moment now and see what these peoples accomplished through the waters of the Red sea and upon the waters easterly of the straits of Bab-el-Mandeb. After Solomon had associated with Hiram, King of Tyre, and Hiram, the son of Abif, the chief of the mechanics who built the temple, and become acquainted with the wealth brought home by Phœnician ships from the great outside world, his spirit of Jewish thrift was excited, and he determined to share in the profits of nautical adventures. In the first book of Kings, chapter 9, verses 26, 27 and 28, we find the following: "And King Solomon made a navy of ships in Ezion Geber, which is beside Eloth, on the shore of the Red Sea, in the land of Edom. And Hiram sent in the navy his servants, shipmen who had knowledge of the sea, with the servants of Solomon.

"And they came to Ophir and fetched from thence gold, four hundred and twenty talents, and brought it to King Solomon." In the 18th chapter of this book, 11th and 12th verses, we find the following: "And the navy also of Hiram that brought gold from Ophir, brought in from Ophir great plenty of almug trees and precious stones, and the king made of the almug trees pillars for the house of the lord and for the king's house, harps also and psalteries for the singers. There came no such almug trees nor were seen unto this day."

In the Second of Chronicles, chapter 9, verses 10 and 11, we find the following: "And the servants also of Hiram and the servants of Solomon, which brought gold from Ophir, brought algum trees and precious stones, and the king made of the algum trees terraces to the house of the lord and to the king's palace, and harps and psalteries for the singers, and there were none such seen before in the land of Judah."

In Second Kings, chapter 10, verse 22, we find the following: "For the king had at sea a navy of Tharshish with the navy of Hiram. Once in three years came the navy of Tharshish bringing gold and silver, ivory and apes and peacocks." This navy of Tharshish is beyond question the navy of big ships manned by Jews and Phœnicians, and the expression here used beyond question is used in the sense we should use in speaking of a navy of big ships, or Baltimore Clippers.

In Second Chronicles, chapter 3, verse 6, we find the following: "And he garnished the house with precious stones for beauty, and the gold was gold of Parvaim."

We will not at the present time stop to ask where was Ophir, where was Parvaim, where did the sailors of Tyre, so skilled in navigation and so capable of navigating the western ocean, as we have seen them to be, as to make successful voyages over to the Orkneys, a distance of some four thousand miles from their homes, spend the three years during which they were absent on their voyages from the easterly gulf of the Red Sea? No Jewish lexicon tells us of almug or algum trees; no Hebrew writer undertakes to describe them. But that enterprising publicist, O'Donovan, who for the purposes of knowledge a few years ago traversed the Caucasus, crossed the Caspian sea and buried himself for two or three years among the still wild tribes of Turkestan, tells us that after his liberation from the Turks, and while traveling in eastern Persia towards the capital, he found a tree which attracted his attention because its fibre reminded him of that of the Lignum Vitæ, which tree the natives called "The Yalgam." Here we have Solomon's algum tree with the name scarcely modified. Would it be the strangest thing that ever happened if these "yalgam," "almug," or "algum" trees, so beautiful as to be unequalled by anything known in Palestine, and for that reason set up as ornaments in God's house, should turn out in the day when all things become known to be rosewood and mahogany from the west coast of Central America, taken on board by Solomon's servants on their return from Parvaim or Peru and the old mines of Potosi, where they had gone for the gold which filled the coffers of Solomon. It may be said that such would be a long voyage; true, but not much longer than a voyage to the Orkneys. Authentic profane history tells us that between six and seven hundred years before the birth of Christ, Pharaoh Necho, King of Egypt, built a fleet in the Red Sea, manned it with Phœnician sailors and sent them out upon the waters to discover the shape and dimensions of the continent of Africa. These sailors passed down through the straits of Bab et Mandel and clear around the Cape of Good Hope and the continent of Africa more than two thousand years before Vasco Degama, and coming in through the straits of Gibraltar after an absence of about two years. Their food supply run low, their supply was mainly wheat, they tied up their ships, landed, plowed the ground with sharpened sticks, cast their bread, not upon the waters, but upon the ground, and thus raised a new crop of wheat, preparing to supply their wants until they should return to Egypt, that eternal land of plenty.

It will be remembered that for centuries previous to the close of the Punic wars under Hannibal the Phœnician people owned and controlled the whole north of Africa, west of Egypt, and the whole of Spain up to the Ebro, and the whole of Cyprus and a very large portion of Sicily, and that when the ancient writers, and even modern writers speak of Spain, the Carthagenians and northern Africa, they refer to the people who sprang from the commercial cities on the eastern shore of the Mediterranean sea, occupying a territory of not more than one hundred miles in extent north and south, and extending back into Syria not more than fifteen miles, whence all these people sprang, and applied to them the general term of Phœnicians.

From the authorities we have quoted we think there can be no doubt but that here and there a learned man among the Greek scholars had come to believe that some eastern navigator had discovered a western world exceedingly productive and beautiful, and that a population of eastern origin had sprung up and existed in the lands so discovered.

IF THE WESTERN CONTINENT HAD REALLY BEEN DISCOVERED ACCIDENTALLY, OR OF SET PURPOSE, WHAT EASTERN NATION WOULD BE MOST LIKELY TO HAVE BEEN THE DISCOVERERS OF THIS WESTERN WORLD.

Nineveh and Babylon are never spoken of as having sent even a keel boat out upon the seas. Egypt has been called the "Cradle of The Arts" and the "Birthplace of Science and Civilization," but Egypt never attained the maritime power or skill to enable her to navigate the waters of the Mediterranean beyond the mouths of her eternal river.

Greece, afterwards so celebrated for science, art and philosophy, was at the day of which Homer sung, a mere association of savage groups, engaged in wars instead of seeking commercial profits in distributing the products of civilized life among the nations of mankind.

And Romulus and Remus had not yet emerged from the sheep folds upon the Italian hills. But very early in the history of the world, and as students of history believe, earlier than the call of Abraham, the interests of mankind had called into existence along the eastern shore of the Mediterranean Sea an active and intelligent population which had engaged in commerce as a means of subsistence, and were carrying it on with such success as was possible in the then condition of the world of mankind. A civilization had sprung up at a very early period along the banks of the united rivers, the Tigris and the Euphrates, and from the Persian gulf to Nineveh and Nimroud, where was produced a great variety of articles of necessity and luxury unknown to the rest of the world. We all understand the story told of Aehan, who secreted in the floor of his tent a Babalonish garment about fourteen hundred years before the Christian era, while Israel was battling against Ai See Joshua, Chap. 8. The children of Japhet had passed up through Persia to the Caucasus, and from the Caucasus around the Black Sea to the waters of the Danube and the Grecian Islands. The luxuries produced in the valley of the Euphrates and the Tigris, called Mesopotamia, furnished a ready basis for a successful commerce across the desert by the way of Damascus to the shores of the Mediterranean; and it was by this means that a commerce sprang up along these shores such as the world had never seen, and which rendered the people resident there the leaders in all the arts of life, including the art of navigation, throughout the then known world, a result but twice paralleled on earth, once in the middle ages at Venice and once in our own age at our magical Chicago. This enabled this people to become the leaders of their race down to about six hundred years before Christ, when there came that terrible war wherein Nebuchadnezzar, by besieging Tyre, caused "every head of that people to become bald and every shoulder to become pealed." Tyre subsisted after the siege of Nebuchadnezzar, but Tyre never attained again the prosperity or influence which she possessed at the commencement of this memorable siege. She had before this time planted two hundred and fifty cities upon the north coast of Africa, including the celebrated city of Carthage. She had settled and occupied two hundred cities in the territory of Spain, and for centuries occupied the whole of that country up to the Ebro. The Jewish historians speak of Spain as Tharshish. Greek writers speak of Spain as Tartesus. Jewish historians and prophets speak of the ships of Tharshish as the most magnificent sea-going crafts known to the world, as we for half of a century boasted of our Baltimore Clipper. Her sailors passed beyond the Pillars of Hercules and passed up the northwest coast of France and established their religion, the worship of Baal, or the sun, among the simple people of Bretagne so firmly and universally that at this day at Carnac, in the Morbihan, there stand more Phœnician funereal monuments of unknown antiquity than can be found together in any form of religion in any other portion of the world's surface. They discovered tin in the Scilly Islands, off the coast of Cornwall, and wrought those mines for centuries. Those Islands were known to the ancient Greeks and Romans as the Cassiterrides, or Tin Islands. They worked both tin and copper mines in Cornwall, and made profits on the sale of the products throughout the known world. They passed up the British channel and through the German Ocean, and in the immense sand dunes at the mouth of the Baltic discovered and utilized that beautiful product of the primeval forests called amber, which they dug from the sand hills. They took with them their priests (the priests of Baal) and introduced the worship of the sun, and made that worship paramount and universal in England, Ireland and Scotland, as well as in Bretagne and the northwest of France. So thoroughly has the religion of Baal been fastened upon the peoples of these regions that portions of them at this day salute the arrival of the Summer Solstice, June twenty-fourth, with burning fires, the precise meaning of which is forgotten, but through those fires in all the early portions of the present century the inhabitants have jumped with their little ones in their arms, as the phrase goes, on Saint John's eve, "for luck." The wizard of the north, Sir Walter Scott, in his song entitled "Hail to the Chief," in the Lady of the Lake, has the following when speaking of "Clan Alpines Pine":

"Ours is no saplin,
Chance sown by the fountain,
Blooming at Beltane," (Baaltime)
"In winter to fade."

Indeed the literary men of Scotland very generally call the Summer Solstice the Beltane. One of the finest of the smaller towns in England even to this day bears the name of Belper, (i. e. Baalpeor.)

They built that wonderful prehistoric open air temple, still standing upon Salsbury Plain, and bearing the name of Stonehenge, the most wonderful monument now standing upon the earth's surface. They built several other circular open air temples in the British Islands, and conspicuously among them, away up in the Orkneys, above Scotland, a very perfect and beautiful one called the "Standing Stones of Stennes."

They visited the Azore Islands, west of Gibraltar, out in the Atlantic ocean, and as we learn by Chateaubriand's Outretombe, Phœnician coin in the last century was found scattered in the soil of these Islands. A man who carries his eyes about him will rarely enter a large Irish assembly, or an assembly of Canadian Frenchmen whose blood comes principally from Bretagne, without noticing here and there a swarthy complexion surrounding intensely bright flashing eyes which speak of Spain and Carthage and the blood of warmer climes.

About one thousand years before Christ, Solomon, the Prince of Israel, resolved to build a temple to the God of Abraham which should exhibit on Mount Zion architectural skill and beauty such as the world had never seen. The construction of that erection was intrusted entirely to the people of Phœnicia; everything was perfected at Tyre so completely that "no hammer or instrument of iron sounded upon the building" after its component parts reached the Mount of God. Even the basins that were to be used in the Lord's house were constructed by the artizans of Phœnicia.

IS THERE ANY EVIDENCE EXISTING UPON THE WESTERN CONTINENT SHOWING OR TENDING TO SHOW WHENCE THE

PEOPLE WHO ERECTED THE PREHISTORIC STRUCTURES ON THE WESTERN CONTINENT CAME?

FIRST.

The soil, climate and productions of the Peninsula of Yucatan, and that part of Mexico and Guatemala where these prehistoric remains are found, are precisely what are described by the European writers who speak of the beauty, the loveliness and the grandeur of the Hesperides and the homes founded by eastern adventurers beyond the western ocean.

SECOND.

The prehistoric structures found in those regions and in neighboring regions are all built on plans and patterns borrowed from lands bordering the Mediterranean Sea, although the structures seem to have followed verbal descriptions rather than exact mechanical patterns.

All of these structures north of Panama seem to have been erected for public purposes, and probably in connection with the offices of some form of religion; and every structure of them, of which any appreciable portion is standing, is built upon or in connection with pyramids as perfectly pyramidal and regularly constructed as were the pyramids of ancient Egypt. Most of these pyramids, however, are mere earth mounds, instead of being constructed of brick or stone as were those upon the banks of the Nile. Let us refer to a few of the localities where these pyramidal structures are most conspicuous.

At Copan, situate at the western border of Honduras, and by the side of the river Copan, is a large enclosure, some two miles in extent, bounded upon the one side by the Copan river, on the bank of which are walls of beautiful cut and fitted stone rising to the height of fifty to one hundred feet, designed to keep the earth upon that side of the river from being carried away by floods. This river at this place constitutes one side of a tract of land laid out nearly in a square, along the outer sides of which, at regular intervals, are constructed, and still remaining, a very large number of pyramids made of hewn stone evidently designed to outline this extended sacred field.

This field within, is ornamented with a wealth of statuary, monuments and figures of idols, practically inconceivable in amount; but we count this statuary of no importance now, as we are confining our attention to the tendency of this prehistoric people to erect pyramids. For a fuller account of this locality we refer to Stephens' Travels in Central America, Chiapas and Yucatan, Vol. 1, Chap. 8.

At Santa Cruz Del Quiche, within the State of Chiapas, Mexico, there exists a pyramid erected for defensive purposes, constructed of earth and terraced as it rises, of enormous proportions; upon its top is a regular fortification upon the top of which rises a pyramidal temple above the fortification. This structure is particularly described by Stephens in the work above quoted, in his second volume, chapter 10, page 161, &c.

At Occasingo in Chiapas, there is a conspicuous pyramid constructed of earth, of somewhat exalted proportions, upon the top of which is a small pyramidal temple having over its porch the ornamentation which is so common upon the temples of ancient Egypt, and occasionally seen in the land of Phœnicia, to wit: a winged globe wrought in stone. The globe itself has become loosened, and has dropped from its place upon the front of the temple but still rests upon the ground before it, while the wing to which it was attached remains in place upon the temple as perfect as when it was first wrought. For a description of these works at Occasingo, see Stephens' second volume, chapter 15, page 258, &c.

The same sort of pyramidal structures remain in admirable preservation conspicuous at Palenque, in Chiapas, where an immense pyramid still exists standing in great perfection with an elegant temple upon its top. Pyramidal structures and shapings are found everywhere at Palenque. See Stephens' Work, above quoted, vol. 2, chap. 20, page 337, &c.

At Uxmal, also in Chiapas, we have another exhibition of pyramidal structures with temples upon their tops. We refer again to the same work of Stephens, vol. 2, chap. 25, page 420, &c.

These remains, to which we have referred, have far greater importance in our investigation than can be attached to the mere building of pyramidal structures. The wealth of sculpture found at the places referred to is immensely great and deserves the attention of scholars and thinking men to an extent greater than we can now devote to them.

In our view, the people who erected those structures possessed a knowledge and civilization far in advance of the population that surrounded them, and that the surrounding populations to a great degree imitated their examples and adopted their religion.

That, as we believe, led to the construction at Cholula, a little town now of ten thousand inhabitants, fifteen miles from Puebla, on the road leading from Vera Cruz to Mexico, on the plains of Anahuac, at the height of 6912 feet above the sea, of that immense pyramid of earth still standing, 177 feet in height, measuring 1445 feet on either side, and ascended by 120 steps.

There are two other pyramids at Otumba, seven leagues north-east of the City of Mexico, and in the language of the aboriginal inhabitants, called, one "The House of the Sun," and the other, "The House of the Moon." The House of the Sun is 680 feet square at the base, and 221 feet high.

On the top of this there was originally erected a great statue of the sun. The other pyramid is much smaller but rises to the height of 144 feet, and on its top was a statue of the moon. Upon the plain about these structures are a number of smaller pyramids not necessary to be described.—The sides of all the pyramids here constructed correspond with the cardinal points of the compas. The pyramids that we have referred to are all patterned after those constructed upon the banks of the Nile, and are all found about the west border of Yucatan, about the north border of Guatamala and south of the centre of the great Republic of Mexico.

It will be well to remember that the mountains and plains of North America cover millions of square miles north and east of the country where these pyramids have been constructed, and that those mountains and plains are covered in many places with earth mounds of an almost inconceivable variety of forms, and yet the form of the pyramid seems to be utterly unknown on the Western Continent, except in the narrow region that we have delineated. We might, perhaps, be justified in asking: From what people on earth could this building of pyramids be copied except from those dwelling upon the banks of the Nile?

THE RELIGIOUS BELIEF OF THE PEOPLES WHO CONSTRUCTED THE WONDERFUL PREHISTORIC TOWERS AND TEMPLES UPON THE CONTINENT OF AMERICA.

They were the worshipers of Baal, the god worshiped by the Phœnicians, and paid their devotions to him with the same rites that they practiced wherever their influence was effective.

It will be remembered that Baal was supposed to exist and was worshiped as a being of biform existence. In his beneficent qualities, as the sun, he was supposed to be the author and sustainer of all life and the fountain of all pleasures. In his sterner character wherein he was known as Moloch or Molech, by the children of Israel, he was the most cruel, stern, relentless monster that the imagination of man ever depicted, and his votaries everywhere sought to conciliate him by presenting him with the most horrid scenes of human agony. Attempts were everywhere made to conciliate him by laying human captives upon his altar, and for want of captives taken in war, such peaceful citizens as the priests saw fit to select.

Human victims were constantly dying upon a thousand altars not only in Phœnicia, but in all western and north-western Europe.

It was firmly believed by the votaries of Moloch that he could be most readily conciliated by the offering of children upon the altars, that he most especially delighted in the sacrifice of the first born of every family. Men thus offering "the fruit of their bodies for the sin of their souls." Early in the history of this worship it was deemed sufficient if children passed through the fires without the destruction of their lives, but down the ages it came to be believed, that if a family would secure the favor of this deity, the oldest child of each union must be actually roasted to conciliate favor. Even good old Abraham who had been called from upper Chaldea to receive all the land of Israel for him and his seed forever, conceived the idea that God required the roasting of the son of Sarah upon the hill of Zion, and never relented until a ray of common sense enlightened his intellectual vision, after he had actually bound Isaac to the altar.

We have referred to the beautiful monuments that still exist at Uxmal, Palenque, Occasingo, Queche and Otumba, and to the temples and monuments still standing there. Upon all these beautiful structures are engraved in the living stone, or wrought in stucco, most striking representations of the sun with a huge priest on either side, standing with arms outstretched each holding in his hands a naked child offering it to the relentless deity. The practice of burning human beings as offerings to the sun existed very extensively down to the date of the Spanish conquest. Showing that the same so-called religion which prevailed in western Europe before the Roman conquest, was still paramount and terribly enforced among these settlers in America, though so far removed from the parent stock. We have spoken thus far of American remains which are found north of the Isthmus of Panama, but there are still existing, in the old land of Peru, structures which for thousands of years have been telling the story of their origin.

There are all over this land of Peru remains not of palaces and temples, but of roads and water-courses showing a mechanical skill such as perhaps cannot be found in any part of the earth elsewhere as existing as early as these must have been constructed.

The people who did this work are absolutely extinct. Many have supposed that in the population of Central America there is still a remainder of the blood of the people who once dwelt there, thus rendering the local inhabitants in some degree superior to the aboriginal Indians of that country. Not so in Peru. It is only from the structures which we find and the conditions which attend them that, any evidence is found that there ever was in Peru, any people superior to the dull Indians of the mountains.

The traditions of the country speak of one Manco Capac appearing in the country at some indefinite period, and that he and his family descendants were rulers for a long course of time, ruling and controling the business and social life of the population of Peru. That blood had been long extinct before the Spanish conquest.

Let us see for a moment whether anything remains to show what were the religious ideas of Manco Capac, and those coming with and descended from him. We find abundant remains of structures and carved columns in the almost desert regions of Atacama, in the high lands of what is now Bolivia, between Peru and Chili, between twelve and thirteen thousand feet above the level of the sea. These structures and carved monuments are largely gathered about the lake of Titicaca. At Sillustani on a promontory extending into that lake, is constructed a stone circle as an outdoor temple, standing more perfect to-day than Stonehenge or Stennes, or the structures at Carnac in Bretagne. It is undoubtedly an outdoor temple for the worship of the sun. See Squires' Travels in the Lands of Incas, page 384, &c.

This, taken by itself, might not prove to a certainty that this outdoor temple was for the worship of the sun, but at Tiahuanuco, in the same work, at page 288 to 292 inclusive, we have the whole story told as plainly as it could be in a thousand printed volumes. Over the entrance to a cemetery is a carved monolith, or single stone, on which is the following described carving: Centrally over the gateway upon this monolith is a well carved figure of the sun, and upon the right hand and the left hand and below, are sculptured some fifty figures of beings with human bodies, and the wings of angels as imagined and represented in western Asia and in Europe. Half of the angels have human bodies, angel wings and the heads of hawks. The Romans and the Greeks held Mercury to be the god of eloquence and of wisdom.

Instead of furnishing him with the wings of the Asiatic angel, they clothed his head in a cap close to the ears with wings extended from the ears, and with other wings extended from his ankles.

It will be remembered that when Paul and Barnabas were upon their great mission through Asia Minor, preaching the gospel, the people became very much excited at Paul's preaching at Lystra and Derbe, and believing that the gods themselves had come to them, they called Barnabas, Jupiter, and the orator Paul, Mercurius. See acts of the Apostles, Chap. 14, 12th verse.

In the Egyptian economy, Thoth was worshiped as the god of wisdom and eloquence, and represented as possessing a human body with a hawk's head. Both regions representing the hawk as the embodiment of wisdom among the feathered creation. Here, at Tiahuanuco, we have the Greek and Egyptian god of wisdom, furnished with the wings of the Asiatic angel, and standing in eternal attendance upon the Phœnician sun god. All these figures are perfect, as showing the ideas and intentions which led to their construction, yet indicating in the roughness of the work that they had been constructed by one who was without exact measurements, probably without patterns, and without the means of obtaining either measurements or patterns. In this cemetery at Tiahuanuco, one will find a hundred structures so like the round towers upon the south coast of Ireland as strongly to awaken one's attention. So that, Manco Capac and his descendants were not only sun worshipers but very strongly imbued with the ideas which originated in the eastern and southern coasts of the Mediterranean sea.

Thus we have seen that the prehistoric people who built the structures in Central America and Mexico, which have in these later days filled the civilized world with wonder and admiration, were constructed by a people whose knowledge of science and the arts had reached the same point of advancement as had been reached upon the banks of the Nile, and in the cities of Phœnicia, for at least a thousand years before the Christian era. That in the erection of these structures they had implicitely followed the patterns, even to their ornamentation, of structures and ornaments then known and adopted in ancient Egypt. That their religious beliefs were identical with those which prevailed among the Phœnician people upon the eastern shores of the Mediterranean sea, upon the coast of north-western Africa and throughout the entire west and north-western portions of Europe. They were sun worshipers, offering infants and full grown human victims to appease the wrath and conciliate the favor of their god. And we have farther seen that that strange people called the Incas, built outdoor temples of standing stones, and upon the entrance to their cemeteries engraved the effigies of the same god worshiped in Central America, and in so large a portion of the eastern world.

So we think we may say, with entire confidence, that it was known to many learned men in ancient times that there were settlements upon the continent of America, and that the dreams of the Western Islands of the Blest, and of the gardens of the Hesperides, rested upon most substantial facts. Modern scholars, looking at the matter casually, have allowed themselves to conclude that, because these discoveries were made at a very early period in the history of the world, by a people who were unable to build their ships according to the rules of modern science, and were compeled to navigate stormy oceans without the aid of steam, and probably without the aid of the mariner's compass, could never have navigated wide seas and stormy oceans.

But how baseless this idea is found to be, when we come to see how easily and successfully the Phœnician people traversed northern, western and eastern oceans, and brought home the products of the whole world to enrich themselves and the peoples among whom Providence had fixed their destinies! And how strangely such a suggestion sounds when addressed to the understanding of peoples who have seen again and again the boisterous Atlantic traversed from continent to continent by three men, two men, and even a single man, in an open boat! So that the origin of this people, who were so conspicuous at one time in Central America, is certainly found to have been of the Phœnicians from Tyre, Sidon or Aridas or from Tharshish or Carthage or the settlements towards the west. The settlement of these countries must have been very early, and their location must have been guarded by all the pains and penalties so graphically described in the ancient authors which we have quoted. Intercourse with Central America from the east must have ceased before the discovery of letters, for nowhere that we have discovered throughout the extent of the American settlements has a letter been found of any form whether Cuniform, Greek, Roman, Hebrew or Phœnician. These western settlers must have been entirely ignorant of Egyptian hieroglyphics, for the figures upon their walls show the invention of a system of hieroglyphics more complicated than anywhere else discovered, and which no Champollion has yet been able to translate. The human mind was not dormant here but its discoveries are utterly lost to mankind. It will be asked what has become of this Central American population who wrought the works in question? This can only be answered from conjecture. The number of actual settlers from the east were doubtless few. In erecting the structures which have been so much admired and wondered at, they doubtless used the labors of untold thousands of the aboriginal inhabitants, appealing perhaps to their fears and desires to conciliate the favor of that God, whose terrors made the Phœnecian priests such an irresistable power over the nations in the west and north of Europe.

But if for a moment superstition lost its terrors, this little flock of more intelligent incomers were powerless to resist the avenging hands of the million aboriginal barbarians. But we are not engaged in discussing the mode in which this people became extinct, but choose to confine ourselves to the questions, who were they, and where did they come from? We say without hesitation, that when Columbus parted from Palos in Spain, he sailed from a Phœnician city, in Phœnician vessels, manned by Phœnician crews to rediscover worlds that the Phœnician ancestors of these men had known and settled not less than three thousand years before. We believe that traditions had always existed in Spain, whose blood up to the Ebro is almost purely Phœnician, of these western worlds discovered by their fathers. No nation north of Spain could be induced to give any considerable attention to the arguments and solicitations of Columbus. True, Ferdinand and Isabella were of northern blood, red haired Goths, but their northern blood had been nourished for a thousand years upon the hillsides of Northern Spain, and they had become Spaniards in fact, with all

Spanish beliefs and tendencies. Beyond all question Columbus took into account the Norwegian and Icelandic voyages and the voyage of Madoc with his Welsh brethren. But Columbus knew that those voyages only claimed to relate to lands lying west and north-west of the Straits of Gibraltar. But when Columbus unfurled his sails outside these Straits, in latitude thirty-five, he made no effort to find the lands claimed to have been discovered by the Icelanders, Norwegians or Welsh, but directed his course to a point from fifteen to twenty degrees farther south, and thus reopened to the knowledge of the world what should have been the happy islands of the west and the storied gardens of the Hesperides. We make no doubt that the Incas of Peru were brought to that country by the ships of the same Phœnician people. But the Incas were very few in number, and came to Peru with mechanical knowledge and the knowledge of pottery far in advance of that possessed by the settlers in Central America, and their works initiated for the purpose of improving water courses and constructing roads were far more beneficial to mankind than the temples erected to Baal in Central America, although the Incas, though more intelligent than the settlers in Central America, were not yet emancipated from belief in that heathen god. Manco Capac, the first Inca, may have been left, for aught we know, by Solomon's fleets from Eziongeber, when in search of rosewood, mahogany, and gold, and may have been one of those skilled mechanics that built Solomon's Temple, and constructed the basins for it, and thus have become enlightened in religious matters, although he had not yet advanced so far as to entirely abandon the worship of Baal.

We are not unaware that Peruvian tradition introduces Capac into Peru at a much later period, but no confidence can be placed in dates suggested by a people utterly unacquainted with letters or figures, and we make no suggestion as to the exact time when the first Inca showed himself in Peru. It may be asked what we are to say in regard to the storied Atlantis, and especially, what shall we say to the fancies of Ignatius Donnelly, who has written such a beautiful romance in regard to that island supposed by him to have existed, and have been the actual birthplace of man. Our reply is that Central America was the only true Atlantis; and that Atlantis sunk in the ocean only when its discoverers became weakened in the face of the barbarous people who surrounded them and lost their supremacy in the commercial world among the nations. Beyond what was true of Central America, Atlantis was a dream of fancy at an age of the world when fancy supplied the place of facts to an uninstructed people.

NOTE.

I am under strong obligations to MR. GEORGE R. HOWELL, Archivist of the New York State Library, for the aid he has given me in selecting from ancient Greek and Roman authors their substantial statements in regard to what they considerered in their day to have been discoveries in the western world.

Milton Keynes UK
Ingram Content Group UK Ltd.
UKHW050244220624
444555UK00005BA/513